A Better Business Today
Small Business Edition

Authored by Paul Sigrist- President of OST Consulting

OST Consulting formulated and implements the Growth Supply and Demand Model when assisting our clients. Within this model we have discovered the impact of innovation and growth (in terms of market share) on the Law of Supply and Demand, each providing a layer of future indicators with increased accuracy.

The Growth Supply and Demand Model was written by Paul Sigrist and Daniel Martin. Any representation otherwise is unlawful, and as such will be prosecuted to the fullest extent of the law. Any republication of the Growth Supply and Demand Model must receive the expressed written consent of the authors.

This book is an educational and promotional tool provided by OST Consulting, in association with our business and distribution partners. "Better Business Today" is a series of books OST Consulting will continue to produce to assist businesses, professionals, individuals, and other categories throughout business to increase efficiency, total output, identify inefficiencies, create more accurate projection models, etc.

Introduction

Most businesses understand that the Law of Supply and Demand dictate their ability to function and sell product. What most businesses, and Wall Street as well for that matter, fail to understand is that innovation and growth are just as important when it comes to measuring functionality, efficiency and projecting sales. Projecting sales, expenses, and other figures within a business based solely off of the Law of Supply and Demand creates inefficiencies.

For those of you who aren't economists, the Law of Supply and Demand is quite simple. The higher the price of the product being sold, the less demand there will be for that given product while the producer of the product is more than willing to produce a high quantity. The lower the price of the product being sold, the greater the demand will be for that given product while the producer will only produce a limited quantity as the reward is limited. The point all businesses strive to achieve is what is called the equilibrium point. The equilibrium point is when the price of the product creates enough demand for the product while incentivizing the producer to supply that same number of units. When supply equals demand, then a business has achieved the equilibrium point. The Law of Supply and Demand has been followed for centuries.

What we have done is proven the correlation between innovation and growth on supply and demand. In today's rapidly expanding technological era, there has never been a more important time to understand this correlation. Understanding and implementing this correlation is what will turn your $50,000 per year business into a $300,000 a year business or more!

The Correlation

This all sounds real nice, right? How is it possible that something that has been relied upon for centuries isn't entirely accurate? Think of it this way, computers weren't even a thought back when the Law of Supply and demand was written. Back in the 60's and early 70's a computer took an entire building to house. The amount of technological and computing power aboard the first Apollo spacecraft was less than the amount of computing power the average smartphone has today. Rapid technological improvements have made this discovery possible.

The correlation between growth and supply is a direct one. If your sales are growing, that allows your to produce more, supply more. Conversely, if your sales are shrinking you don't have as many resources available to provide goods for sale. This seems simple enough. However, if you want to be able to measure your business against the competition you can't use sales. To compare yourself against competitors, use market share. If we only used sales to measure growth, we wouldn't be able to account for discounts, profit margin, or various other factors. By using market share, we can identify a plethora of resourceful information. Which business has more customers, a more loyal customer base, more pricing power, etc. etc. Using market share is key when measuring growth of a business, your business.

What spurs growth? More specifically, what spurs growth of market share? Increasing market share means there is an increased demand for your product. How do you increase demand for your product in today's marketplace? Innovation. Innovation is a tricky word. Most people would read innovation and assume we are only referring to technology. That would be the furthest thing from the truth. Innovation implies a multitude of items. Personnel, product(s), marketing, packaging, R&D all constitute different variations of innovation. Innovation by definition means "the act of starting something for the first time". In this case the act of operating or functioning differently represents innovation.

How can personnel, marketing, or packaging represent innovation? Remember that innovation implies doing something differently. Innovation can be a bad thing or a good thing. It is up to each individual business to determine which methods to employ. An innovative approach to personnel could be as simple as paying a higher wage. Higher wages typically create happier workers and a healthier work environment. Happier workers and work environments create a better atmosphere for customers, which in turn drives additional sales. That is just one type of innovation for personnel.

Marketing innovation can be created by having the catchiest or most viral ads. Perhaps you want to offer something to potential customers that no other business offers. That would be a form of innovation. The best packaging, a quicker form of shipping, superior management, elite inventory management systems, these are all forms of innovation. Creating more innovation increases the demand for your product. More demand means increased potential sales and increased total revenue.

You Against The Competition

Now that we understand just how big of a role growth and innovation play in your business directly, what do we do with this information? How is a business owner or manager supposed to use this information to better the business? The key in all of this is to constantly compare your numbers against the competition. Let's be fair. If not for the competition, you would have no challengers and sales would be through the roof. Alternatively, if not for your business they would be on top of the world. Right?

When looking at both growth and innovation, compare your levels against local competition, regional competition, then industry standards. If you are spending the same amount of resources on innovation as your competition, we know that your competitor will have more desirable products or services. More desirable products from your competition mean less sales for you. Lack of spending on innovation over the course of several years could very well lead to irrelevance for your business as you fall further and further behind industry standards. Look at the cellphone market today. How many flip phones do you see compared to smart phones? Many, many cellphone makers have gone out of business because they didn't spend enough on innovation to keep up with the change in technology.

When looking at growth, the same holds true. It wouldn't be prudent to compare your business to the entire industry if you own and operate a local fruit stand. It also wouldn't be prudent to compare yourself to the competition of a single city if you are an international conglomerate. Most cities, counties, and states track how much each industry produces within it's borders on an annual basis. Depending on how large your company is, compare yourself appropriately. We find that once you break through the $1,000,000 in sales mark, depending on your industry naturally, it would be wise to move from the city level to county level of competitor comparisons. Likewise, moving above the $10,000,000 mark would warrant a move from county to state comparisons. This all depends on where your company is conducting business. A retailer in the state of Montana would have far lesser thresholds than a retailer in New York, L.A., or Chicago simply because of population and total output of those cities and the states with which they reside in.

Let us review an example briefly. If Company A and Company X both produce and sell the same types of products and services, they would be considered direct competitors. If Company A has a market share of 10% within the city and spends $.30 per $1 of total revenue on innovation; Company X has a market share of 30% within the city and spends $.05 per $1 of total revenue on innovation, we see a few things. Company A has a market share less than Company X. To gain more market share, Company A is spending three times that of Company X on innovation. With these numbers before us, we can determine that Company X will eventually lose market share to Company A because of that innovation spending. Likewise, we see that Company X could prevent Company A from overtaking it by increasing innovation spending.

Since Company X has more market share, we know that they have more revenue coming in. More revenue means that they could afford to spend slightly less on a per dollar of total revenue basis to keep up with innovation by Company A. Since Company X has three times the market share of Company A, Company X only needs to spend one third of what Company A spends on a per dollar of revenue basis. Since Company A is spending $.30 per dollar of revenue and Company X is spending $.05 per dollar of revenue, we see that Company A is actually spending six times more than Company A. We have already established that Company X needs to spend one third of what Company A does on innovation because of the difference in market share, so that means that Company X would need to spend $.10 per dollar of revenue on innovation to keep pace with Company A.

Naturally, Company X could spend $.20 per dollar of revenue to dwarf Company A's expenditure on innovation because of the difference in market share. If Company X were to spend $.20 with a 30% market share and Company A spent $.30 with 10% market share, we would see that Company X is actually spending three times that of Company A on innovation. That difference would continue to widen the gap in market share between Company X and Company A. Considering a business can't devote every penny on innovation because of the costs of conducting business (i.e. payroll, rent, utilities, inventory, etc.) this could be a fatal blow to Company A. Company A would be forced in to one of two options: Close their doors; or sell products at lower prices to recapture market share.

Personnel Decisions

By this point, we should all understand just how important innovation is to a business. For small businesses, innovation is especially important. We've all seen just how quickly different smartphone apps shoot to stardom and fall from grace. In today's day and age of extremely rapid technological advances, the majority of apps have a small window of opportunity for profitability. This small window also applies to personnel within a small business.

More often than not, a small business owner or manager will have a brief phone conversation with an applicant followed by an interview that may last an hour or two. That's it. That is all the time you as a business owner or manager have to evaluate an individual to fill a role within your company. That time is especially critical to evaluate what that person can bring to your organization. In the current job market that individual may be available for a period of a year or more if you reconsider, but in a healthy economy that person may only last a week or a mere day or two.

This may be an opportune time to use Andrew Carnegie as a prime example of how to fill your employee ranks within your business. Andrew Carnegie created the largest steel company in the world. He built it from nothing to the point where he was one of the richest and most powerful people in the entire world, not just the United States. He could never have done that if he hadn't surrounded himself with the correct people.

See, Carnegie was competing against the likes of J.D. Rockefeller and J.P. Morgan to become the richest person in the United States. His competitors had a killer instinct and remarkable business prowess. Carnegie knew he lacked that killer instinct, and he also knew he needed to increase his profit margins if his company were to allow Carnegie to overtake J.P Morgan and Rockefeller as the richest man in the United States.

How did Carnegie increase his profit margins? He increased his innovation. Carnegie sought out someone who was an absolute ruthless businessman, Henry Frick. Henry Frick was known for taking any means necessary to achieve the results he desired. Henry Frick was hired as Chairman of Carnegie Steel Company. With this new appointment, Carnegie Steel began drastically increasing innovation. Frick implemented longer work days, switching from eight to twelve hour shifts, while simultaneously slashing wages.

Carnegie Steel was already the largest steel company in the world with dominant market share before Frick. With Frick as Chairman of the company, he increased innovation drastically and consequently further increased market share. When an industry market share leader continually increases innovation, this forces the entire industry to increase their innovation levels to keep pace. From a consumer standpoint, this action typically creates lower prices and better goods or services.

Keep this in mind when you are making your personnel decisions. When you as a small business owner or manager are interviewing that potential new addition to your company's ranks, very rarely should you look for someone who is an exact duplicate of yourself. Remember that innovation is key. Someone who thinks and operates differently than you do offers a completely different perspective across the spectrum. Carnegie, arguably one of the most brilliant business people in American History, couldn't decipher how to increase profit margins by himself. He recognized that and brought in someone who thought and operated completely differently, and consequently Carnegie Steel ushered in an era of unprecedented levels of production, profit margins, and total revenue.

There is no need to reinvent the wheel. Take a page from Andrew Carnegie. Take a page from Henry Ford, Steve Jobs, and countless other innovators. Identifying your strengths is one thing. Identifying your weaknesses is even better. One of the most prudent things a business can do is reward employees who offer increased innovation. Remember, innovation can present itself by thinking or operating differently or more efficiently. An employee who is able to complete a task in thirty minutes is more valuable than an employee who completes the same task in forty minutes at the same level of quality. That is a simple example of innovation, or doing things differently.

How does compensating an employee more than another employee impact your company's budget? More specifically, how does a business owner or manager take that compensation into account when we think in terms of innovation? We should look to an example to understand this.

Suzy is paid $10.00 per hour and is able to complete her daily tasks in just four hours. Billy is paid $8.00 per hour and is able to complete his daily tasks in eight hours. Suzy's pay accounts for $.011 of each item sold. Billy's pay accounts for $.01 of each item sold. How in the world do we decipher the impact on innovation spending for the business?

Break down all of this information. We determine innovation spending as a product of the total revenue from products sold minus all non-innovation expenses. In this case we can keep all things equal except the difference in labor efficiency and the cost each employee has per item sold. Let's do the math.

We see that Suzy is able to complete the same tasks as Billy in just 50% of the time. Suzy completes the tasks in four hours, and Billy completes the tasks in eight hours. Excellent! Suzy is compensated at $10.00 per hour and accounts for $.011 in expense per item sold. Billy is compensated at $8.00 per hour and accounts for $.01 in expense per item sold. We see here that Suzy makes 25% more than Billy, and that she accounts for 10% more expense per item sold.

Confused yet? That's alright. We purposely gave you more information than you needed. As a small business owner or manager you typically have or are given more information than you need, right? Suzy makes $.001 more than Billy on a per item sold basis. Suzy accounts for

$.011 per item sold in terms of expense, while Billy accounts for $.01 per item sold in terms of expense. Suzy's impact on innovation spending would be that difference, or $.001.

You compensating Billy and Suzy at different amounts only impacts the expense each carry as it relates to each item sold. Seeing that Suzy is 50% more efficient than Billy in her ability to complete the same tasks tells you that she would be worth up to 50% more than Billy on an expense per item sold basis. Since Suzy is only compensated 10% more than Billy in terms of expense per item sold sold, you know that your business is getting a phenomenal deal.

The fact that Suzy makes 25% more than Billy has a very real impact on the bottom line. There is no debating that fact. However, that difference in hourly pay has no impact on innovation spending. Hourly pay has no direct correlation towards items sold. Instead, look at the cost each employee has in terms of per item sold. By doing that we can quickly come to the conclusion that Suzy's increased productivity and efficiency more than warrants her additional 10% cost per item sold. As a business owner or manager, you should be very happy to spend the $.001 on innovation to have someone like Suzy versus Billy.

Too Much Of A Good Thing

Thus far we have been preaching innovation, innovation, innovation. Bear in mind that too much of a good thing can be problematic as well. Go back to our previous example of Company A and Company X. Depending on profit margins, it could be argued that Company A spending $.30 per dollar of revenue on innovation is too much. In order for Company A to have a chance at justifying spending $.30 per dollar of revenue on innovation, Company A needs to enjoy having at least $.30 per dollar of revenue in profit after all other costs are accounted for.

If Company A only enjoyed $.29 per dollar of revenue after all other costs and still spent $.30 on innovation, what does that mean? There are only two options available:

1- Lower innovation expense to $.29 per dollar of revenue or less.

2- Increase prices to adjust for the overage in innovation spending.

That may seem like common sense, but surprisingly even giant corporations don't account for this difference appropriately. Let's again take a look at the smartphone market. With a new product offering, the smartphone, profit margins for the first makers of the smartphone were through the roof. Market share was also through the roof. However, to create such an innovative product, the expenses to develop the smartphone were forcing those first smartphone producers to charge higher prices to recover the research and development and marketing expenses.

What happens if Company B comes to the marketplace with a product for $100 and dominates the marketplace? Company Z takes note of that growing marketplace and product and releases their own version to sell for just $50. While the profit margin for Company Z is less than Company B, Company Z is able to take market share away from Company B. Even with lower profit margins, the increased market share allows

Company Z to enjoy a higher level of total revenue and possibly greater profits.

The tactic employed by Company Z is a commonly used form of market penetration called "undercutting". Undercutting happens quite often in high growth markets as companies enter a price war to claim more market share. Companies like Company B from our example open themselves up to competition undercutting them in the marketplace. By allowing innovation expenses to increase past the profit per dollar of revenue threshold, companies are forced to raise the prices on products to account for that innovation expense. To be the first to market with a given product, this tactic could be the best option depending on your competition.

If being first to market isn't important to your business, a competitor has already beaten you to the market, or your business simply doesn't have the available resources to be the first to market, it would be wise to implement the undercutting technique. Undercutting typically provides lower innovation expense, which allows the business to sell products for a lower price than the competitor who was first to the marketplace. Bear in mind, this assumes the products are extremely similar or like in nature. With minimal differences between products, consumers will be more inclined to acquire the item of lesser cost to them.

This is also why you typically don't see extremely high profit margins with more mature products and markets. Mature products and markets have already endured pricing wars. Mature products and markets have already gone through what we call the innovation cycle. Due to the decreased cost and familiarity of the matured product, consumers are drawn to the product that provides the most quality for the available dollars they have.

With the innovation becoming negligible across a mature industry, the only way to influence demand from the consumer is through incentives. Wait. Aren't incentives a form of innovation? In fact they are. Remember, when we discuss innovation we aren't speaking directly to

R&D or a product exclusively. Innovation takes many different forms.

Mature industries use incentives such as coupons or cash back offers to

claim market share. While implementing these measures may cause a

business to suffer smaller profit margins or even a deficit in the short-term,

in the long-term the business enjoys increased profit margins after the

incentives have concluded through increased market share.

Incentives, otherwise known as innovation via marketing, are a

popular strategy used by many of the largest companies and industries in

the world to attempt to gain market share. When profit margins are well

defined across an industry due to the mature nature of the product offers,

market share is key. Again, too many incentives will directly impact profit

margins and possibly the profitability for businesses. In an attempt to

regain consumers after the financial and housing meltdowns, luxury

brands have been using incentives to drive consumer demand. In the

short-term the luxury brands are experiencing shrinking profit margins, but

in the long-term these luxury brands will enjoy increased consumer

demand.

As a small business, incentives such as giveaways, coupons, or other deals will help drive consumer demand and raise awareness of your product. It is imperative that those incentives be accounted for not only in the marketing budget, but the innovation budget as well. Balance is key. Too much of a good thing still has a negative impact. While your brand and total sales may increase in the short-term, profitability will also be adversely impacted. Bear in mind that for every metric of innovation the business should enjoy an increase in market share equal to that innovation. If the gain in market share is less than innovation, your business has allocated too many resources towards innovation. If the gain in market share is greater than innovation, your business has not allocated enough resources towards innovation. That is simple supply and demand. Think of the correlation in the same breath.

A Win Win Scenario

As for forecasting future sales and developing projections, this way of conducting business is far more accurate than other methods. The Growth Supply and Demand Model that we have discussed throughout the book gives your business an extreme advantage as we have described. An increase in market share shifts the supply curve on the Law of Supply and Demand to the right, a loss of market share shifts the supply curve to the left. An increase in innovation expenditure shifts the demand curve to the right on the Law of Supply and Demand, a decrease in innovation expenditure shifts the demand curve to the left. In layman's terms, if market share and innovation decrease the business won't be able to sell or supply as many products. If market share and innovation increase the business will be able to sell and supply more products.

Innovation and growth (in terms of market share) are exceedingly important for businesses, no matter their size. In terms of small business, it is imperative that the correlation between innovation and growth are understood and implemented. Misunderstanding the correlation could lead to disastrous results. Always remember that for every metric of innovation, there should be an equal metric of growth. If there is an imbalance, there needs to be an adjustment made to innovation expenses. Also, without innovation there can be no growth. Innovation directly impacts demand for your products. Growth directly impacts how much a business can supply to the consumer. Without growth, there can be no increase in total sales.

OST Consulting developed and implements this Growth Supply and Demand Model for all of our clients when analyzing their business practices. Make sure to keep an eye out for our next installment in this series of E-Booklets. We will be providing you with greater insight into how to use this Growth Supply and Demand Model for managers, sales, personal life, and many other uses. As always, make sure to LIKE OST Consulting on Facebook. OST Consulting is here to help your business grow and succeed, and we look forward to donating a portion of

all our proceeds to promoting the small business movement.